POTTY TRAINING

I Can Do It, So You Can

To:

From:

Hello! My name is Mia
I love to run and play

but I always need my diaper changed
at the start of every day.

I can feed myself
at breakfast

and brush my teeth
as well.

I know which clothes
I like to wear.

But I don't like
my diaper's smell.

Mom and Dad bought me a present,
it's in a great big box.
I ask Daddy, "What is it?"
He joked, "A pair of socks."

Daddy gets some scissors out
and starts to cut the tape.
Soon I'll get to see inside,
then I can tell its shape.

Soon the box is open.
Daddy lifts it out real steady.
I try to work out what it is.
A hat for on my heady?

It could be a new storage box
to put my toys inside.

Or maybe it's a new toy boat
To sail on the ocean tide.

I peek down at my diaper.
It fits me nice and snug,
except when full of pee or poop.
I give the waist a tug.

My parents use a potty,
so maybe I'll try too.
Then I won't need a diaper
that's wet and stinky poo.

My diaper comes off quickly
when I want to poop or pee.
Then I sit on my potty,
Peggy sits right next to me.

I run when I need potty.

But, sometimes I am too late!

Some days I read Peggy a book...
...as I sit and wait!

Woops! I had an accident!
I almost start to cry,
Dad says, "Mia, that's okay,
At least we know you try."

Mom gives me some new pants to wear,
The other's were so wet.
She says, "Don't worry Mia,
You must not give up yet!"

One night I jump up out of bed,
and whisper quietly to my Peggy,

I need to use the potty now,
I know this time I'm ready!

I quickly pull my diaper off,
Peggy sits upon my lap,

I sit there waiting for a bit...
and then I laugh and clap!

look inside the potty,
And there is poop and pee,
I didn't mess my diaper,
I yell, "Hooray for me!"

"Mom and Dad, I did it!
excitedly I cried,
My parents are both smiling
and so happy that I tried!

Bye-bye diaper, go away,
There's no more need for you.

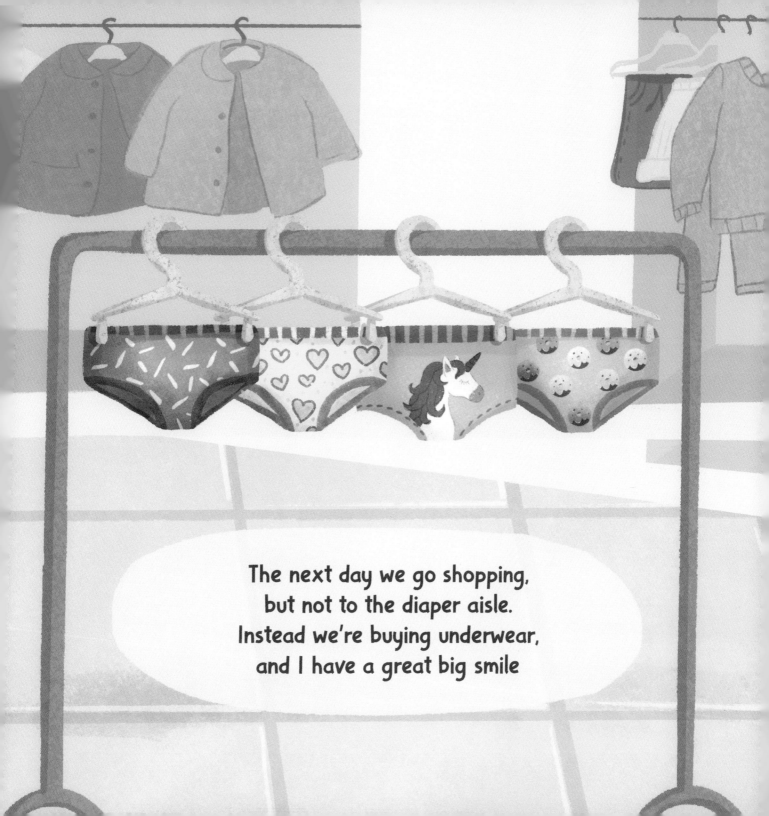

The next day we go shopping,
but not to the diaper aisle.
Instead we're buying underwear,
and I have a great big smile

I'm a big girl now, you know
I can play and jump and run.

No wet and smelly diaper
is going to spoil my fun.

Do you want to know a secret?

You can ditch that diaper too.
You'll have fun using the potty
just like Peggy and I do.

Now I'm off to use the potty,
no more diapers for me, ever!
I am cleaner and much happier,
and I feel so proud and clever.

What Did You Think of POTTY TRAINING?

First of all, thank you for purchasing this book POTTY TRAINING.
I know you could have picked any number of books to read,
but you picked this book and for that I am extremely grateful.

I hope that it added at value and quality to your everyday life.
If so, it would be really nice if you could share this book with your friends
and family by posting to Facebook and Twitter.

If you enjoyed this book and found some benefit in reading this,
I'd like to hear from you and hope that you could take some time to post
a review on Amazon. Your feedback and support will help this author
to greatly improve his writing craft for future projects and make
this book even better.
I want you, the reader, to know that your review is very important.
I wish you all the best in your future success!

Scan Me

Get your free potty training checklist and coloring pages on the link:
natiarty.com/pottygift

Printed in Great Britain
by Amazon